# MARVEL
# CAPTAIN AMERICA™

## AN ORIGIN STORY

# PaRragon

Bath · New York · Cologne · Melbourne · Delhi
Hong Kong · Shenzhen · Singapore

Long ago, a peaceful little island sat just off the mainland of a place that was called different things by all the different nations of people who lived there.

As time went on, more and more people came to the little island.

They wanted to leave behind the lives they led in a place known as the Old World, and build new ones in a place where they believed anything was possible.

For most, this island was the first stop on the path to a new life in this young nation.

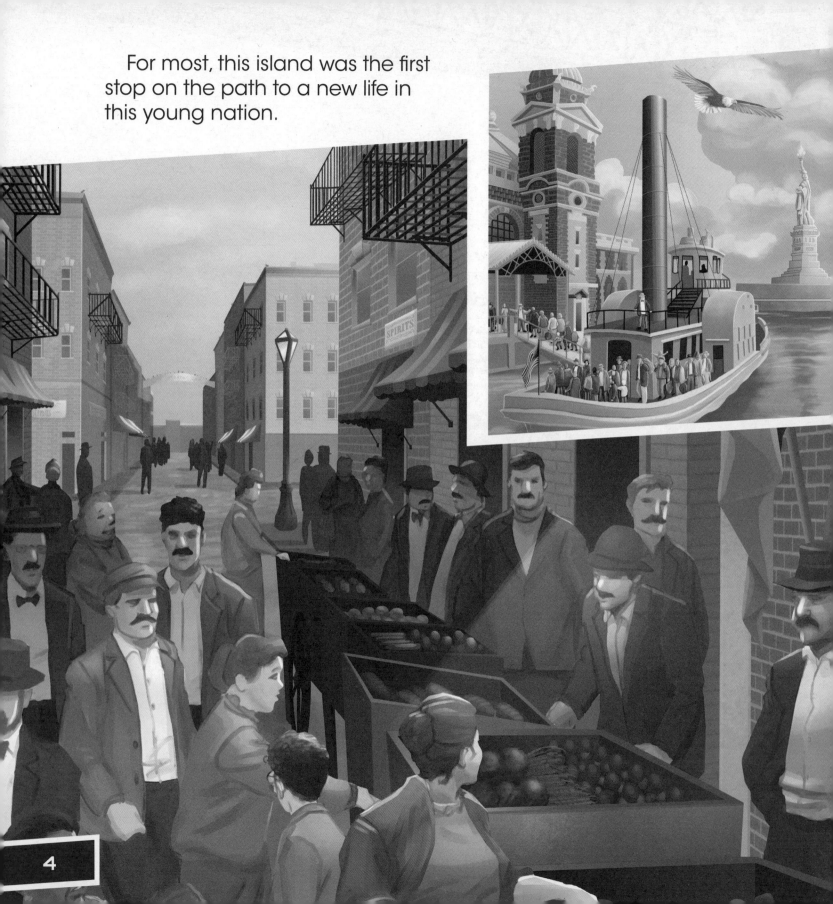

This island was known as Manhattan, in the city of New York. And the country would become known as the United States of America – or America, for short.

Before America was even 200 years old, it was called upon to fight alongside other countries in a terrible war that was destroying the world.

The news of war moved people. It seemed like everyone in the country wanted to join the army to help. Including a young man named Steve Rogers.

Steve had been upset about the war for some time. Now that America was involved, he could do something about it.

Steve waited his turn. Every man so far had passed.

Steve was confident he would, too.

But the doctor told Steve that he was in no shape to join the army. Then he told him that there was another way to get into the army. He handed Steve a file marked:

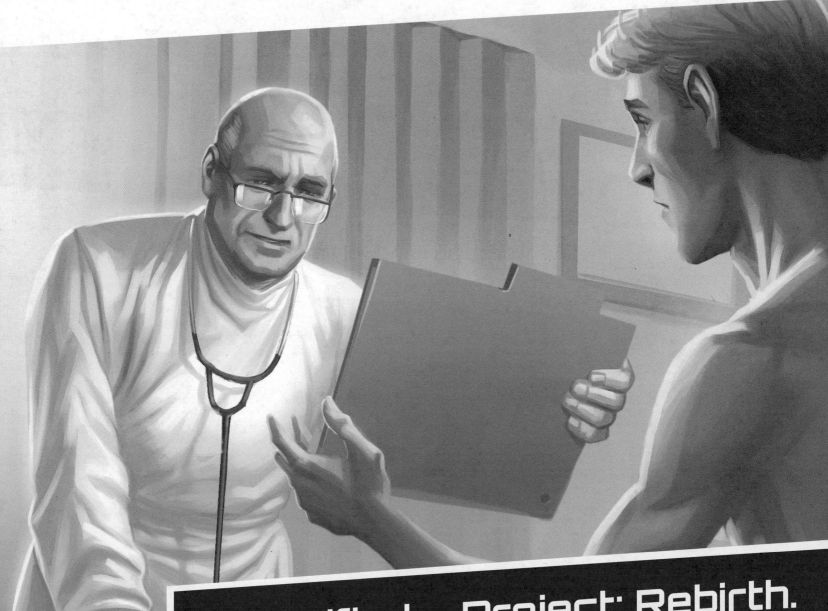

Classified – Project: Rebirth.

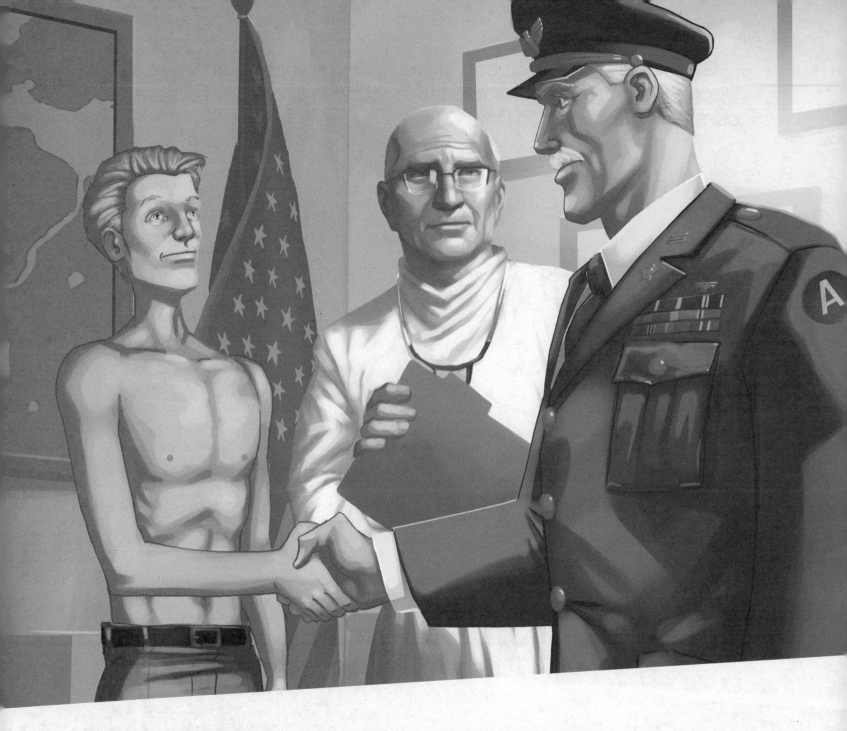

The doctor told Steve that if the experiment worked, he would be able to join the army after all.

Steve said he would try anything to become a soldier.

The doctor called in a general named Chester Phillips. The General was in charge of Project: Rebirth.

General Phillips introduced Steve to the project's lead scientist, Doctor Erskine. The doctor told Steve that the Super-Soldier serum, combined with the Vita-Rays …

... would transform him from frail and sickly into America's

# FIRST AVENGER!

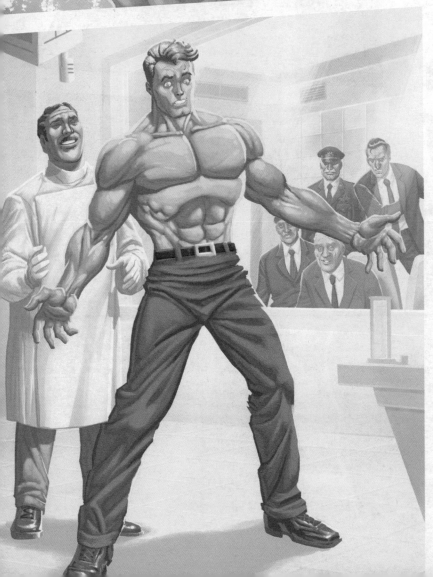

The experiment was a SUCCESS!

But before Steve, General Phillips or anyone else in the lab could notice, an enemy spy who had been working in the lab suddenly attacked! He did not want the Americans to have such power! The doctor was hurt and unable to copy the serum.

But Steve, in his new Super-Soldier body, was safe.
The army put Steve through a very special training camp
to teach him how to use his new body.

The general presented Steve with a special shield made of the strongest metal known and a unique costume to help Steve mask his identity.

With the costume and shield, Steve would now be known as America's most powerful soldier ...

Captain America!

Captain America's missions were often dangerous. In order to keep his secret safe, the general asked Steve to pretend to be a clumsy army private.

But when no one was looking, Steve donned his costume and fought for justice.

Steve's reputation as a clumsy guy meant he was often moved between units.

This allowed Captain America to fight on many different fronts of the worldwide war!

No one ever suspected that the worst private in the US Army was also the best soldier that the army had!

# BUGLE
FINAL

## TANK NO MATCH FOR CAP!

FINAL

Captain America kept on fighting for liberty, until finally ... the war was won.

Though the country might not always live up to its promises, Steve vowed to protect America and its ideals: justice, equality, freedom ...

... and the dream of what the nation he loved could accomplish.